John Shaw Billings

Ninth annual report of the officers of the Detroit House of

Correction to the Common Council of the City of Detroit, for the

year 1870

John Shaw Billings

Ninth annual report of the officers of the Detroit House of Correction to the Common Council of the City of Detroit, for the year 1870

ISBN/EAN: 9783742812858

Manufactured in Europe, USA, Canada, Australia, Japa

Cover: Foto ©ninafisch / pixelio.de

Manufactured and distributed by brebook publishing software (www.brebook.com)

John Shaw Billings

Ninth annual report of the officers of the Detroit House of Correction to the Common Council of the City of Detroit, for the year 1870

REPORT

OF

INSPECTORS OF THE HOUSE OF CORRECTION

TO THE

COMMON COUNCIL.

To the Honorable Common Council of the City of Detroit:

The undersigned, Inspectors of the Detroit House of Correction, have the honor to transmit to you the ninth report of the Superintendent of that Institution, together with the reports of the Teachers, Chaplain and Physician.

The report of the Superintendent is very full, and we shall forbear any attempt to abstract the same. But we do not hesitate to say that a more interesting and important report has never been laid before you. We believe it worthy of your most careful attention, and of that of all persons interested in an enlightened prison discipline.

The net earnings of the past year, over and above the expenses, were $5,324.64—an amount smaller than the previous year, but not unsatisfactory, when we consider that nearly all business has been depressed during the past year. The manufacture of boots and shoes had been successfully initiated in the Prison. The Prison buildings and grounds had not only been kept up, but improved. And though the debt of the Institution, for the supply of material necessary for the carrying on of its manufactures, was larger than is desirable, we hoped this would soon disappear under the successful working of the system.

Unfortunately the very last night of the year brought us the calamity of a fire which destroyed the entire west line of workshops, the tools and stock therein, with the steam engine and boilers.   The loss over insurance is about $13,000, and there must also be considerable loss from the partial suspension of the manufactures of the Prison.   Energetic measures were at once taken to restore the portions of the buildings destroyed, with greater capacity and facilities for future operations.   Full details on this subject will be found in the report.

The sanitary condition of the Prison during the year has been entirely satisfactory.

But we call your especial attention to what has been done towards the instruction of the prisoners, and for their moral and intellectual cultivation.   The results seem in the highest degree encouraging, and we respectfully suggest whether farther and more systematic efforts in this direction should not be undertaken.   Much credit is due the gentlemen whose voluntary labors in this respect have produced so valuable results.

We also invite your attention to the careful and instructive discussion, found in the Superintendent's report, of the subject of *indeterminate sentences.*   There is no question that *some* change is needed.   In many cases our present system of short and determinate sentences is absolutely pernicious.   What is the true remedy may, perhaps, not be so clear.   But no one, we think, can doubt that a confirmed drunkard, or a confirmed prostitute, should no more be let loose in society than an insane person.   They are, from the very nature of the case, proper *wards* of society and the law; and until they can be restored to society with a fair prospect that they will not endanger its safety, its peace and its purity, and will not further pursue their courses of self-destruction, they have no claim whatever to be delivered from this wardship.   The same is probably true of every case of crime, where the criminal exhibits a settled proclivity to a life of crime.   Restraint from vice and crime, even though compulsory, is not a wrong.   And if the restraint is not carried beyond what is necessary, it is a blessing, both to the subject of it and to the public at large.   Care, of course, should be taken to guard against every possible abuse of undue confinment under indeterminate sentences; and it is believed that this can be satisfactorily done. We are glad that the subject is now so fully brought before the public, and we hope that a full consideration of it will result in a great improvement of our present system.

The same high order of discipline and the same attention to ·perfect cleanliness has been maintained as hitherto.

We earnestly hope and believe that with the restoration of our work-shops, with the increased facilities afforded, with the aid of the experience acquired, and with such improvement as may be expected from wise legislation, the Detroit House of Correction will win even greater reputation as a model prison.

WM. W. WHEATON, *Mayor,*
GEO. V. N. LOTHROP.
N. W. BROOKS,
L. M. MASON.
Inspectors of the House of Correction.

DETROIT, February 14, 1871.

SUPERINTENDENT'S REPORT.

To the Board of Inspectors:

GENTLEMEN—The ninth annual report of the Superintendent of the Detroit House of Correction, together with those of the Teachers, the Chaplain, and the Physician, I now have the honor to hand you.

THE RECENT FIRE,

Which occurred at 6½ o'clock on the 31st of December, 1870, the date of this report, formed the subject of an official communication to the Common Council very soon thereafter, and your Board were acquainted with the particulars of it immediately. It is proper however to state in this report that the fire started in the boiler-room, which was supposed to be secure, and though it was discovered before very great progress had been made, still, through a series of unfortunate and unforseen circumstances, we were unable to extinguish it until the west line of workshops and their contents of stock in process, machinery and tools were entirely destroyed or ruined, and the boilers and engine damaged to the amount of $2,000, the engine being rendered unfit for further use.

The value of the contents thus destroyed is ascertained by an inventory and appraisal, just completed for the basis of my annual report of the financial result of the year in this department, to be $19,013.26, and the value of the building, as ascertained by the appraisers of the Insurance companies, is $6,100, making a total of property destroyed of $25,113.26.

The exposed portions of the House of Correction buildings and manufacturing material were insured to the amount of $45,625, of which $12,000 was written upon the building and property destroyed. The loss therefore over and above the insurance, will be **$13,113.26,** though a larger sum than this will be required to build the new and enlarged building, engine, and purchase machinery as is proposed. The estimated cost of the building and engine alone (which are in process of construction at this writing, 20th January), is $15,000, and it is expected that the manufacturing operations will be fully under way by the 1st of April next. Nevertheless the probable loss from this suspension so long, will be a serious drawback upon the results for a year or two to come. There is no doubt but the effect of this accident will be speedily and fully overcome, that the industrial department will again, as in the past, yield a sufficient support without drawing upon the public purse, but it is probable that some assistance will be needed by the way of loans or appropriations while we are bearing the full force of the present consequences. This leads me to state particularly as to the

FINANCES.

The House of Correction owes at this date, in notes and accounts, $54,144.83, and there are outstanding valid accounts in favor of the institution to the amount of $31,934.85, showing a balance of indebtedness of $22,209.98, to which should be added the item of cash overdrawn $2,676.78, making $24,886.76.

From the statement of property *before the fire*, which statement is based upon a very low valuation, it will be seen that we have an amount in the aggregate $91,499.81, available of course, *when converted*, to liquidate the above balance, and even *after the fire* the amount is $72,486.55, as will be seen from the statement entitled " summary," from which also the precise standing of all liabilities and assets will clearly appear. You will observe that the House of Correction is in good financial condition except as it is affected by the calamity of fire above alluded to. The indebtedness, though large, had and now has abundant assets to to meet it, when these can be turned, and the whole was entirely in hand until the accident occurred. The earnings for 1870 have again exceeded the expenses by a handsome though somewhat reduced figure, and after deducting the loss on machinery, tools and stock by the fire, and the deficit for the first two years, we still show a surplus of earnings over all deficits and losses for the whole period of the institution of $68,149.21.

The results of the past year's financial operations are stated, exclusive of the effects thereon from the before mentioned fire, in the detailed statement of this report, and may be summed up as follows, namely : The whole amount of expenditure is $66,- 176.24 ; the earnings are $71,400.88 ; showing a balance gained of $5,324.64. The expenditure is nearly the same as for 1869, differing only $446.25, though the several general items of expenditure include greater variation. Thus, the general expense account for 1870 is $4,796.10 larger, the increase being chiefly for fuel and lights rendered necessary by the use of the additional apartments erected in 1869, and by the undersize and worn condition of the engine, requiring therefore much more fuel than will be needed for the new one in process of construction. Clothing and bedding account is $1,493.29 less, which is attributable to the good quality of the cloth purchased last year, and to a somewhat reduced number of inmates during the latter part of 1870. I judge this reduced number of prisoners may have been somewhat effected by the more liberal bestowment of gratuities to them on their release, for the expenditure for discharged prisoners account is $1,365.44, or $489.93 in excess of that for 1869. Repairs account is for 1870 more than for 1869 by $1,829.49; for a full analysis see the tables of this report. The whole establishment is kept in the best of order by this considerable annual expenditure from the earnings, which is doubtless true economy; but the best judgment of men conversant with this subject warrants such expenditure as is required to maintain a handsome appearance of the grounds and the buildings outside and inside for its effect in cultivating a right public sentiment as to the treatment of prisoners, and for the influence exerted upon the prisoners themselves, and in this opinion I concur. The considerable sum paid for interest this year grows out of an accumulation of manufacturing material, amounting at date to $69,685.75; this placed us in the most favorable position for a profitable year's work in 1871, and the advantage is not entirely neutralized by the loss of a part of it by fire. The large stock of material is necessary to insure the uninterrupted employment of the prisoners, which is a basis of all the good results we aim at. The profits for 1871 would have reduced the interest account for that year if no accident had occurred, but this cannot now be hoped. The amount of doubtful debts carried to suspense account for 1870 is $3,986.52 less than for 1869; the larger amount last year was made up mostly of an item against Wayne county, which the Common Council declined to authorize you to collect. The amount of doubtful accounts for 1870 is $1,286.17, on sales in the aggregate $146,153.42, the loss being less than one per cent on the gross amount of sales. The House of Shelter account is $1,756.02 less than last year, owing to the smaller number of inmates and the temporary closing of the House in October last, which is subsequently explained in this report. Provision account, Insurance account, and Furniture and Fixtures account, are each slightly less than for 1869, but the variation is so small that comment is unnecessary.

There is also a diminished *income* for 1870, it being $8,198.82 less than last year; $1,516.66 of the difference is in Board account, and arises from the smaller number of prisoners received from Wayne county, namely, 114 *less* than for 1869; the remainder of the difference is in Chair account, caused by the reduction of prices made on the 1st of February, 1870. It will be noticed that the Shoe shop opened in April last has earned $2,112.59 net. From the statement " *Cash, Debts and Property,*" you will observe that the sum of $6,995.26 has been expended for permanent improvements and charged to Stock account as follows, viz.:

To complete the North Wing.....................................$5,007 58
For additional steam heating apparatus,........................ 467 84
For the shipping house protection and platforms,............... 288 52
For concrete roadway and gravel for roads and walks,........... 764 89
For increasing the heighth of the guard wall, etc.,............ 466 43

　　　　　　　　　　　　　　　　　　　　　　　　　　　$6,995 26

The year past has been an unfavorable one for business generally, and has affected us by necessitating a reduction of the price for chairs, the employment of traveling agents to sell, the extension of credits in both time and amount, and in the greater delays and difficulties of collecting. But, on the whole, this annual review of the transactions of the business department of the

House of Correction, though showing only $5,224.64 for the balance of earnings over the expenses, seems to me quite satisfactory, and all that could be reasonably expected under the circumstances.

Probably no large private business establishment in the country, certainly no prison of this class, was ever commenced and carried forward so many years as the House of Correction has been in existence, with more immunity from accident or financial embarrassment than we have had; and notwithstanding the loss by fire and the difficulties growing out of it, I am confident that within two years we shall be again financially independent, and that no serious hindrance will occur at all to the progress of the important reformatory work so surely going forward, or to the influence of the institution in promoting "Reformatory Discipline and Penitentiary Reform." The department to which I would now invite your attention,

THE EDUCATION OF ADULT PRISONERS,

Sentenced for short terms, was entered upon vigorously in this institution two years ago, and favorably mentioned in my last report, but mentioned as an experiment. It has proved so successful as to lose the uncertainty of an experiment, and become an established department of the system of administration adopted here, and is as indispensable to the objects we aim to accomplish, as the sanitary and industrial divisions, or the ministrations of religion. I know of no more valuable contribution to prison literature than the brief reports of the teachers of the prison schools, viz; Prof. H. S. Tarbell and Miss Emma A. Hall, and their value consists in the facts they contain and their clear statement of them. The whole number of prisoners enrolled in the school during the year is 612; their great need of education is indicated by the fact that after the progress made in the school for a greater or less time, until the date of this report, their condition as compared with children in the public schools, is viz:

16 per cent. as those of the Primary Grade.
20 per cent. as those of the Secondary Grade.
50 per cent. as those of the Senior Grade.
14 per cent. as those of the Senior and more advanced.

The progress made by the pupils still further reveals by contrast their deplorable condition as to education when admitted, which progress both teachers state to be about an average of *two and a-half years* of common school work, accomplished by the prisoners in *one year* here of only 84 sessions, two and a-half hours each. Or it may be stated thus: They accomplished in *forty-two* school-days (drawn out over a year of time) as much progress in books as the average scholar in common schools in *five hundred* school-days. If with such rapid progress maintained for a time, only the point stated is reached, how deficient they must have been when admitted; and if such interest and success is possible, how desirable it is that prisoners should have the advantages of a good school. To communicate to you as clearly as possible the effects of our educational means upon character, I beg leave to reproduce from the language of the teachers. Mr. Tarbell says, " It is hard to place upon paper any adequate view of the plainly discernable change, which no figures can show, in the bearing of the men, their awakened desire for knowledge and self-culture, and their increased susceptibility to intellectual and moral truth." Miss Hall says she observes "A gradually increased activity of mind and ability to think, a higher type of library books are chosen and more intelligently read, there is a better and more critical reception of the lectures, addresses and readings given them, and a perceptible seeking for practical helps to a better life."

The course of lectures for 1870 have been of unusual service to the prisoners, partly because of their better ability to appreciate them, and partly from the well selected subjects of the lectures and their skillful presentation. That some true idea of this influence may be conveyed, I will state the date, lecturer, and subject of each lecture during the year, viz:

11 March.....................................REV. W. HOGARTH, D. D.,
  The Nobility of Work.

10 March...................................D. B. DUFFIELD, ESQ.,
  The Beautiful.

26 March......................................PROF. J. M. B. SILL,
  Heat.

2 April...REV. J. M. ARNOLD,
  Flowers.

9 April.....................................REV. W. R. G. MELLEN,
  The Labor Question.

16 April.............................. ....REV. A. T. PIERSON,
  The History of Alphabetic Writing.

23 April.....................................HON. E. C. WALKER,
  The Ocean and its Inhabitants.

7 May.....................................PROF. DUANE DOTY,
  The Amazon and its Valley.

21 May.....................................HON. C. I. WALKER,
  The power of the individual to affect civilization and the reflex influence. (An historical sketch).

28 May.....................................HON. J. L. CHIPMAN,
  The Restraints of Law are Good.

11 June.....................................PROF. C. A. KENT,
  How to do Business.

18 June.....................................REV. GEO. WORTHINGTON,
  Ancient Architecture.

20 August.....................................MR. C. BUNCHER,
  Reading, from Dickens.

27 August.....................................WAU-SEE-KEE,
  The Prison System and some of the Social Habits in China.

3 September.....................................J. F. CONOVER, ESQ.,
  Humorous Poetry.

17 September.....................................D. R. SHIRE, ESQ.,
  Temperance and Intemperance ; my own experience.

24 September.....................................PROF. FREDERICK STEARNS,
  Chemical Combinations of Bread.

1 October.....................................MR. C. BUNCHER,
  Reading, from Dickens.

8 October .....................................SUPERINTENDENT,
  Reading, Courage.

22 October.....................................PROF. GRIFFITH,
  Vocal Power, with illustrations.

29 October.....................................REV. W. HOGARTH, D. D.,
  Self-Conquest.

12 November.....................................PROF. D. P. MAYHEW
  Definitions, Man.

19 November.....................................Mr. C. BUNCHER
  Reading, Selections Grave and Gay.

26 November..PROF. D. P. MAYHEW,
    Methods of the Mind.

3 December.................................... PROF. C. A. KENT,
    The Control of the Emotions by the Will.

10 December......................................PROF. D. P. MAYHEW,
    Mnemonics.

17 December....................................C. M. DAVISON, ESQ.,
    Money and Banking.

24 December...Mr. C. BUNCHER,
    Reading, Dickens' Christmas Carol.

24 December..MRS. WETMORE, HUNT, TROWBRIDGE, and Mr. WHEELER,
    Musical.

31 December......................................PROF. D. P. MAYHEW,
    Mnemonics.

I cannot express the feeling of gratitude and encouragement that comes with the writing of the above array of names, but desire to put into this report at least a hearty acknowledgment of the value of the services rendered. All these lectures and readings were carefully prepared and forcibly delivered, and nearly all of them were worthy of any audience that assembles in our public halls to listen to lectures. They have served to stimulate and elevate the minds of prisoners and officers, thus raising the House of Correction to a higher social atmosphere, adding force to its reformatory efficiency.

The most interesting experiment and remarkable success in oral instruction to uneducated adults, of which I have known, is that of Prof. D. P. Mayhew's lectures in mental science to the prisoners here. He has succeeded beyond all expectations in captivating the minds before him and in actually accomplishing in them a systematic course of thought for the hour at least. These lectures vary in length from an hour to an hour and a-half holding to the end the undivided attention of the whole audience. Some of the most valuable moral precepts are inculcated "by the way" and in the very wide field of illustration with which Prof. Mayhew's mind is stored.

That such gentlemen should take time to prepare and deliver such lectures to prisoners, as they have blessed us with during the past year, is an omen full of promise for an improved public sentiment on the whole subject of crime and its punishment, and that at no very remote point of time.

It is certainly to be regretted that the opportunity and helps to somewhat of education and the progress so surely began should be terminated and often obliterated by the old worn-out practice of predetermining the precise date for the prisoner's release. This practice also deprives about one-half of our prisoners of these privileges because of their short sentence, and is also a hindrance to the others, for it is harder to arouse their interest in the matter to begin with.

The protection of society from crimes involves the reformation of prisoners (or their continued control), and reformation involves education up to a given point of development in each case, which *cannot be* without authority to hold the prisoner in contact with educational means until the result is reached.

THE HOUSE OF SHELTER.

This department of the House of Correction was opened in October, 1868, remained in full operation until October of this year, a period of two years, when it was temporarily closed and has not yet been reopened. It was closed (temporarily) for the reasons (1), that the interior of the whole building needed renovation, which required the labor of workmen, whose presence prevents that perfection of order and privacy of family life so essential to the welfare of the women under treatment here; (2), who, with one exception, were prepared to go to situations provided for them, and there were no new cases in the House of Correction ready to transfer, and none on the " discharge list," for release before this date, who were proper subjects for this department. Thus, practically we were without material to mould. But if this were not so, or if it had seemed desirable to seek subjects among the abandoned who have not been committed to the House of Correction, this was impracticable for (3), Mrs. Wigin, the principal matron, had signified her intention to vacate her position, to assume duties of a different nature elsewhere, and therefore, it was desirable to take this course.

The needed repairs have been made, the whole establishment without and within is as good as new, indeed in much better condition than when first completed, and no considerable repairs are likely to be needed for years to come. While the loss of Mrs. Wigin's services is severely felt (for she possessed very extraordinary abilities for a work of this kind), still this alone would not delay the reopening of the House, were there a sufficient number of cases at hand whose reformation by this means might be reasonably hoped. The whole number of females now in the House of Correction is considerably less than at any time since the House of Shelter was opened, and of these there are less who seem susceptible of benefit from their *voluntary* residence at the House of Shelter; indeed, there are none who could be safely transferred there, or at least not enough to work the system and warrant the expense of maintaining the department for that purpose. But there are *thirty* (a number equal to the full capacity of the House of Shelter), who could be transferred at once, and successfully treated, if they were committed to custody, so as to give some measure of control until a cure is really wrought, and the House thus full would produce nearly or quite sufficient income to defray the current expenses. This cannot be done, however, without such changes in the law as have been urged in the former reports; changes it is hoped the Legislature will make at its session this year, giving time and opportunity to carry the reformatory process, often so certainly begun, to a point of probable perfection.

It is not true, as is commonly believed, that strong religious influences, upon these persons, produce in a brief space of time such reformation as fits them for society, and insures their rectitude of mind and conduct for ever after. Nor is it true that (as a class) they possess the *power* to pursue persistingly a proper course, even when the purpose so to do has been really formed. Neither is it true, in any general sense, that persons living vicious or degraded lives *desire* to escape therefrom, that they will fly to find a respectable place if only opportunity offers. These three current views or some one of them will be found to underlie almost all organizations for reforming fallen men and women, and though they may find confirmation in isolated cases or seem to succeed for a time, I aver that they are false as the rule, and need to be eradicated from the public mind. The reformation of such involves often a radical change in the native tendencies of the mind, or, when this is impossible, such developed self-control as shall hold these tendencies in subjection to the reason and the will, together with a more favorable situation in society when fitted and restored to it. That this process cannot be had unless continued control is conferred is evident to the casual reader even. The necessary changes require an improved bodily condition, that diseases may be healed, the physical man toned up and refined, that the intellect shall be stimulated and developed until the mind actually sees the truth, takes the true view of the best policy, and trains in improved company; also, that the religious faculties assert themselves, responding to genuine goodness, having reverence for the good Father of us all, and a right feeling of fellowship for the good of our kind. This is *cultivation*, demanding time not only, but unremitted contact with the agencies for systematic training; contact, to which these cannot hold themselves, nor can they be held without legal authority, and that for indeterminate duration, except as it is terminated by the improvement in each case. As was stated in my report last year, " the House of Shelter, and similar homes elsewhere, doubtless supply much needed humanizing means, afford a refuge and a friend for despised, friendless victims of society; but do not, cannot reach the evil that makes them a necessity, nor accomplish general reformatory results, without such changes of law as are suggested." The foregoing views are induced from my life-long observation, reflection, and particularly from the experience of the past two years in the conduct of this House of Shelter Department. If they are sound, and the system for treating prisoners in our city and state could be based upon them, the House of Shelter expenditure would be fully repaid by the benefits derived. However, the House of Shelter is worth its cost for work it will do; whether the desired change in the law is had or not, it will satisfy our benevolent impulses, and save the necessity and *the stigma* of turning back to the scorn and severity of so called Christian society, poor homeless orphan girls, penniless and a prey to the vile; and it is worth all it cost for what has already been done for those who have been members of the family.

There have been 61 women treated here, all but two of whom have been released, most of them being sent to situations; the two still in custody are returned to the House of Correction. From recent information we learn that 24 are positively doing well and their future is hopeful; 24 we have lost track of, many of whom were "repeaters," but are now away from our city at least, and of three of them there is some hope; 4 are still under legal control and are therefore hopeful cases; 7 are living improperly we learn, and 2 are doubtful. Fifty per cent. of the cases treated are *now* doing well; thirty women who were so far abandoned as to be imprisoned are now, with more or less of effort, striving for an honest living and respectable station. I am sure these all could be saved if we had still some measure of authority over them; as it is we are powerless to aid, and can only *hope* for the best. The great contrast between the present situation and character of some individuals who were admitted to our establishments two years ago, degraded and despairing, is calculated to enkindle enthusiasm, but I am not, and ought not to be satisfied with this or the general result stated; these successes embolden the outlines of defeat, which suggests new means or methods, deeply impressing upon us all the great importance of *right principles* as the basis of the system; while the success achieved encourages and enables us to go forward with the work.

With the exception noted, the principles upon which the House of Shelter is organized and conducted *are sound;* this is demonstrated beyond question. *Cultivation*—Christian culture, will elevate the low and save the lost. A home, a personal friend of refined type, and education, are successful means, but it is an indispensable condition of general success that the Matron shall have at least *parental authority* over her family. Therefore, I would earnestly urge that your attention be directed to procure the passage of the bill which you have seen, as the true ground of greater usefulness for the House of Shelter Department and for the whole House of Correction.

2

The reduced number of females in the House of Correction, and particularly of those who are suitable for the House of Shelter is partly attributable to the decision of the Supreme Court by which the operation of Sec. 4, of Act 145, passed in 1869, popularly known as

THE THREE YEARS' LAW,

was limited to the county of Wayne. The practical effect of this has been to stop all proceedings under the act itself.

This decision, added to the unpopularity of the law among such persons as sometimes compose police court juries, who either misapprehend the true spirit of the law, or fail to discover the turpitude and injury to society from the offense it names, or disregarding these considerations and finding their pecuniary interest immediately promoted by vice, refuse to render a verdict of guilty even when the evidence is reasonably clear. I believe the first count in the above indictment of some jurors is the true cause of the difficulty alluded to, and that the misapprehension arises from the maximum limit named in the law, viz: three years. They seem obtuse to the other provisions by which the time is reduced, the benevolent design being obscured by the words *three years*. It is believed the law would be very differently esteemed by people who do not study laws closely if there were no maximum time limit affixed, if the commitment should be *until reformed*—rendered respectable. More favorable feeling would also be promoted by changing the phraseology of the sentence to "The Board of Guardians," instead of imprisonment in any prison establishment. These ideas are embodied in the bill before mentioned.

From my report last year it will be seen that on the 1st of January, 1870, there were in custody under the "three years' law," seventeen females, as follows: in the House of Correction proper, thirteen ; in the House of Shelter Department thereof, three; conditionally released at service in the country, one. During 1870 only one was received under this law, which (if added) makes the whole number who have been under treatment this year, to be eighteen. Twelve of these were peremptorily released in February (an effect of the Supreme Court decision before mentioned). One who at the begeining of the year was under conditional release, was absolutely released on the 8th of April, having in nine months improved sufficiently to warrant this action, as is confirmed by her respectability at this time. One a mere child, sentenced to the House of Shelter until she should attain the age of twenty-one years, received 23d December, was absolutely released on the 21st of June, 1870, being then returned to her parents in New Jersey, with whom communication had been previously had. Four only now remain. The present situation of these is as follows: One, who was received 26th of July, 1869, transferred to the Shelter 11th of October, conditionally released 7th of May, 1870, is still at service doing well, has accumulated quite a sum of money, deposited to her credit in Savings Bank, is hopeful, encouraged, and her self-respect much stimulated, but it is not deemed wise to release her from guardianship yet. This girl had been several times imprisoned for short periods without beneficial effect, and her present promising prospects are undoubtedly traceable to the principles of this law. If there were no declared limit to our guardianship, a complete cure in this case might now be surely predicted. Another received 26th of August, 1869, is still under regular control and culture in the House of Correction. She, like the one just named, had been several times recommitted, and not until April, 1870, was there any appearance of improvement; since then it has been slow but steady and sure. It has been found quite impossible to rid this girl's mind of the impression that she is sentenced for *three years*, the maximum limit named in her commitment, which has proven a hindrance in the early stage of treatment, and will be likely to divert the mind again when the time of release draws near. The third was received 27th of December, 1869, removed to the Shelter 19th of May, 1870, but returned to the House of Correction 12th of September. The sentence of this girl is until she reaches her majority, she being now under fifteen years of age. This is a case of *kleptomania*, which accounts for her return to the House of Correction and present detention there. She has been motherless from infancy, is of weak mind naturally, and has had bad associations. Years of culture and a life-time of kind control are re-

quired to save her from a life of crime.   The fourth and last
prisoner received and remaining under this act, was admitted
12th of January, 1870, is of French origin, 26 years of age, and
has served several sentences here.   It is difficult to conceive and
of.doubtful propriety to explain the deplorable condition of this
woman when received.   The body was thoroughly diseased, the
eyes being nearly blind, indifference pervaded the mind, and no
indications of moral sense could be discovered.   Some improvement has been made, which will have reached a point of respectable progress by the time she must be released according to the
sentence, then to be arrested and progress of an opposite nature
occur and continue until she is again committed to custody or
until death ensues.

These four cases must show   (1). That more time is required
to effect a cure and protect society from the influence of such
persons than is ordinarily given under a determinate sentence,
or than *can* be conferred under existing laws.   (2). That the
limit of three years, or any time limit, is likely to thwart the purpose of protection, and prevent personal reformation.   (3). That
the popular idea of imprisonment for *punishment* has so taken
hold of the public mind, so pervades our laws and their administration, that the placing of vicious and criminal persons under
curative control cannot be accomplished by the courts so long as
the sentence has the *appearance* of undue severity, whatever may
be its benevolent purpose.   Is not the true remedy for these difficulties the one already indicated, and will not the principle
apply to *all* the offenders who come into the House of Correction,
whether male or female.   I refer of course to the remedy of

THE INDETERMINATE OR REFORMATORY SENTENCE.

The principles and practical operation of the proposed measure
will best appear from the bill which has been prepared for presentation to the Legislature as follows, viz:

AN ACT proposed in addition to the acts relating to the Detroit House
of Correction, and to prevent crime by the restraint and reformation of
offenders.

SECTION 1. The People of the State of Michigan enact: That any
person who shall be convicted of any offense punishable by imprisonment

in the Detroit House of Correction, and who may be sentenced to imprisonment therein under any law now in force or hereafter to be enacted, shall be and are hereby constituted wards of the State, and subject to the custody and control of the Board of Guardians, as hereafter provided by this act.

The Circuit Judge of the County of Wayne for the time being, together with the Inspectors of the Detroit House of Correction, shall constitute and be denominated the Board of Guardians, whose power and duties shall be as further provided by this act, and said Circuit Judge shall *ex officio* be Chairman of said Board.

SEC. 2. All Courts of Record having criminal jurisdiction in the State of Michigan, and all Police Justices and Justices of the Peace in said State, who, under the provisions of law, may sentence offenders against the criminal law to confinement in the Detroit House of Correction, in the exercise of their criminal jurisdiction, shall sentence all offenders convicted before them,.or any of them, of any offense now or hereafter made punishable by imprisonment in the Detroit House of Correction, to the custody of the Board of Guardians aforesaid, but shall not fix upon, state or determine any definite period of time for the continuance of such custody ; provided, that in cases of assault and battery of which Justices of the Peace have jurisdiction, fines may be imposed in accordance with existing laws ; and provided further, that this section shall not be construed to take away any power to suspend sentence, that said Courts and Justices may have ; and in case of such suspended sentence the Courts or Justices before whom such offenders may have been convicted, may at any time cause the re-arrest of such offenders for the purpose of having such suspended sentence pronounced and executed.

The Court or magistrate imposing such sentence shall in such case furnish the sheriff or other proper officer a copy of the complaint, information or indictment upon which such conviction is had, a statement of the defendant's plea, the names and residences of the witnesses sworn in the cause, an abstract of the testimony given, the sentence rendered and the date thereof, which copy, statement and abstract, signed by the magistrate or clerk of the Court, shall be delivered to the Superintendent with the prisoner, and shall be *prima facie* evidence against the prisoner in all proceedings for the release of said prisoner by writ of *habeas corpus* or otherwise.

It is hereby made the duty of any sheriff, constable or policeman to convey forthwith such persons so sentenced to the Detroit House of Correction, and deliver them into the custody of the Superintendent thereof, for which services and all necessary expenses, he shall receive such compensation as may be allowed by the Board of Supervisors of the County where such conviction is had.

The Superintendent of the Detroit House of Correction is hereby required to receive all persons so sentenced and delivered, to detain them subject to the authority of the Board of Guardians, and to release them as said Board may direct.

The following form of commitment of prisoners sentenced as aforesaid, shall be sufficient authority for the officer to transfer, and for the Superintendent of said House of Correction to receive and detain, such prisoners ;

...........County *ss.* To..........of the..........of..........and the Superintendent of the Detroit House of Correction. Greeting: *Whereas,* after trial upon a complaint duly taken by me............of .... in said County, was convicted of............and was by me sentenced to be imprisoned in the Detroit House of Correction, in the custody of the Board of Guardians of said House of Correction. *Now, therefore,* you ....of the............of............are hereby required to convey said............to said House of Correction and deliver............ into the custody of the Superintendent thereof, and you, the said Superintendent of said House of Correction, are commanded to receive said ....into your custody and......safely keep until discharged in accordance with law.

Given under my hand at the............of............this....day of ......A. D. 18..

SEC. 3. The said Board of Guardians shall have power to detain in the House of Correction. subject to the rules and regulations thereof, all wards committed to their custody, power to establish rules and regulations under which such wards may, upon showing evidence of improved character, be absolutely or conditionally released from confinement in said House, or from other guardianship, custody and control ; power to resume such control and custody wholly or in part, and to re-commit to said House any ward at any time prior to their absolute release.

The written order of said Board of Guardians, signed by the Secretary thereof, shall be due authority for any member of said Board or their agent, any sheriff, constable or policeman, to arrest and return any ward not heretofore absolutely discharged, to the custody of said Board in said House ; and it is hereby made the duty of all sheriffs or other officers as aforesaid to execute such order, the same as it is now their duty to execute ordinary legal process.

SEC. 4. It shall be the duty of said Board of Guardians to maintain such minimum of control over all wards committed to their custody under this act as shall prevent them from committing crime, best secure their self-support, and accomplish their reformation.

The said Board shall actively undertake the reformation of the wards aforesaid, by means of culture calculated to develope right purposes and self-control, and by granting them social privileges under such social and legal restraints and influences as will best cultivate right purposes and promote correct conduct, when this may be done with safety.

When any ward shall be received into said Detroit House of Correction, said Board of Guardians shall cause to be entered in a special register the name, age, nativity, nationality and parentage of such ward, with such other facts as can be ascertained, indicating the constitutional tendencies and propensities, the social influences connected with the early life, and based upon these an estimate of the present condition of such ward and the best probable plan of treatment.

Upon such register shall be entered quarter-yearly or oftener, minutes of observed improvement or deterioration of character, and notes as to the method and treatment employed ; also all orders or alterations affecting the standing or situation of such ward, the circumstances of the final release, and any subsequent facts of the personal history which may be brought to their knowledge. An abstract of the record in each case remaining under their control shall be made semi-annually, submitted to the Board at a regular meeting thereof, and filed with the County Clerk of Wayne county, which abstract shall show the date of admission, the age, the then present situation, whether in said House or elsewhere, whether and how much improvement has been made, and the particular reason for release or continued custody as the case may be.

The Board of Guardians shall establish rules and regulations by which any ward may have the privilege to see and converse with the said Board of Guardians quarter-yearly at least.

When it appears to the said Board that there is a strong or reasonable probability that any ward possesses a sincere purpose to become a good citizen, and the requisite moral power and self control to live at liberty without violating law, and that such ward will become a fair member of society, then they shall issue to such ward an absolute release, but no petition or other form of application for the release of any ward made by any person whatever, based upon any ground save that herein stated, shall be entertained or considered by the said Board.

SEC. 5. If any person, through oversight or otherwise, be sentenced to confinement in said House of Correction for a definite period, said sentence shall not for that reason be void, but the person sentenced shall be entitled to the benefit and subject to the liabilities of this act, in the same manner and to the same extent as if the sentence had been in the terms required by section two of this act, and in such cases said Board of Guardians shall serve upon such ward a copy of this act, and written information of their said relations to said Board.

SEC. 6. All Acts and parts of Acts inconsistent with the provisions of this Act are hereby repealed.

Objections to this measure have been suggested. (1). That it places under the control of the Board of Guardians the liberty of the offender, without predetermined and peremptory

time limit. This is an objection to the principle of indeterminate sentence.

The question, whether the liberty (so called) of offenders
against the law shall be abridged, is to be decided by the courts
and not by the Board at all; but, when restraint is deemed
necessary by the Magistrate or the Court, the question as to the
kind and duration of it, it is proposed to leave to the Board of
Guardians. The Board, like the courts, will be charged with
the duty of protecting society from further infractions of law
by such persons as having once violated it are convicted and by
competent courts placed in their custody. Whether the Board or
the Courts can best accomplish this is a matter to consider.

I aver that under the present system as administered, society
is not protected in any just sense, but that crime keeps pace
with the growth of population or outstrips it, the several
grades of crime maintaining substantially the same proportion
to each other, year after year, one decade with another; and
that prisoners committed to penitentiaries and reformatories are
not (as the rule) reformed, but pursue for life, save when restrained, the same style of living, exert the same kind of influence - individual instances of reform never so touchingly told to
the contrary notwithstanding. This is a necessary concomi-
tant of the present system (though some improvement may be
made), for the following reasons: (*a*). The punishment which
civilized society will permit upon offenders cannot be made
sure enough and severe enough to intimidate and thus to deter
the classes who are criminally inclined; and, since a determinate
sentence conveys inevitably the idea of retribution, if not of
retaliation, it places the law and those who feel its restraints in
a position of antagonism, the one to the other; tending thus to
stimulate and increase those conditions of the public mind favorable for the practice of crimes. For, it is from an appreciation
of the benevolent design of law, the friendliness of its provisions, that the people are summoned to its support and remain
obedient subjects. (*b*). Persons *must* be released at the expiration of a determinate sentence, whether they have become better
or worse; and if by any possibility they improve while imprisoned, the process must end at a definite date or be greatly

endangered by the necessary and sudden change of circumstances involved, or by the absence of subsequent guardianship. The definite time stated also hinders improvement, by putting into the mind a bad element; for if the sentence appears to the prisoner as less than he deserved or expected, he is led to esteem his offense as of less importance than formerly; if too great, he is likely to think himself a hero with his class, and to be embittered by what seems to him arbitrary and unjust treatment; but if the sentence imposed just meets his own view, still he feels that the service and suffering patiently endured works absolution without regard to changes of character, that may or may not have been wrought. Experience teaches that to inform prisoners of the date of their prospective release is to supply an absorbent for natural healthy mental processes, and that their attention, so difficult to attract and retain at best, is enchained in counting and contemplating the passing time that brings nearer the certainty of their release.

The regularity of crimes proves the existence of causes that may be ascertained and brought in contact with counter agents. If, under the present system of sentences, no diminution of the ratio of crimes has occurred, it can hardly be expected in the future, and there is much reason to believe that the system itself is a cause of the crimes it seeks to cure; it is therefore a pertinent inquiry whether and what changes shall be made, etc. It is here proposed to try the experiment of *restraining convicted persons until they can be safely released ;* this is the sum and substance of the indeterminate or reformatory sentence plan. Can anything be more reasonable?

But (2) objections are offered, not only to the principle involved but of a practical nature. It is thought that persons may be committed for mere piccadilloes, and be restrained longer than is deemed just (by Mrs. Grundy), for the offense committed; or, that those who commit more heinous crimes will be released too soon, violating thus the "public sense of justice," and destroying the alleged deterrent effect of punishment; or, that with the best design and most faithful administration on the part of the Board of Guardians, it will be impossible to judge accurately; or, that such great responsibility and power will open the Board to improper influences, affecting their action.

If it is supposable that the Board of Guardians are as honest and intelligent as the justices of the peace and other officers who now determine (within prescribed limits of course) the duration of imprisonment in prisons or reformatories, of which they can know little or nothing, and over which they have no control, then it will not be doubted that the Board who control the establishment, prescribe the *regime*, and frequently observe the effect of means employed, will be more likely to judge right as to the interests of society by way of prevention, and of the interests of prisoner by way of reformation; so that under the proposed change improvement in this particular is probable.

The bill provides for such records and returns, such examinations and intercourse between the Board and the prisoner, that it is quite impossible that carelessness or forgetfulness as to any prisoner shall occur.

The fear that the perpetrators of serious offenses may be released so soon as to destroy the deterrent effect of public punishment has been already answered. The fear that they will be so released as to violate the popular judgment as to justice, and thus precipitate lynchings, is, it seems to me, chimerical. Lynchings usually spring from a sense of inadequate provision of the law for penalty, which pertains to statutory *limits*, not to the unlimited penalties. This imagined result must come, if at all, from mal-administration; but is not likely to occur, for the public attention is usually turned from criminals when they are placed in safe custody. Who ever heard of the lynching of a pardoned prisoner or for fear he would be pardoned? If violence is incited by improper administration of the Board, it is not certainly a necessary result of the proposed system, and may be remedied by appointing a new Board, and by a better administration.

The first objection of this practical series is trivial, and I will not occupy space with a reply, except to say that often very bad characters can only be convicted of venial crimes, in which case they ought to be so restrained as to prevent the greater ones. This suggests the value of the law as a *preventive* of crime, but I refrain, for I am only answering objections that have been made.

If properly administered it is expected the following benefits will be derived from the law.

It will help educate right sentiments as to the benevolent nature of law and the curative design of its penalties. The certainty and continuance of restraint authorized, will exert the largest possible deterrant effect, and preventive benefit will be derived from the thorough treatment of vagrants and the various classes who are propagators of criminals and crimes. The minds of prisoners will be at once concentrated upon the reformatory object of their restraint, and their co-operation secured. Errors constantly occurring in the imposition of penalties upon first offenders and others may and will be speedily corrected. Prisoners will be released at the right time, at the best place and under the most favorable circumstances, with such guardianship afterwards maintained as shall do the most possible good for "discharged prisoners" who are now so sadly neglected.

That the law *will* be wisely administered seems probable, for the responsibility resting upon the Board will make the office of Guardian an honorable one, and being without pecuniary profit will probably be filled by good and competent men. The joint duty of determining the duration of imprisonment, and the kind of treatment applied, will insure their careful attention to their work, and being known as the sole authority for this purpose, their action will be closely scrutinized, and they will be held to the rigid accountability such as justices of the peace and courts scattered all over the state are not and cannot be. The advantage of experience and opportunity to observe the character of prisoners over that possessed by the courts affords very strong probability of improvement and wise judgment, and possessing the power to rearrest those who return to vicious associations or practices after their conditional release, the Board holds in its own hand the ability to correct any mistakes they may make.

That errors will occur is not denied or doubted, *but at the worst* the proposed plan must be an improvement upon the present one, and since it is only proposed to try the experiment at the Detroit

House of Correction, under the direction of the Board named in this bill, which is made up of gentlemen whose character and intelligence are all that can be desired, and since the experiment is for the purpose of arriving at the truth, it is hoped the bill may become a law.

CONCLUSION.

Respectfully commending to your notice the satisfactory sanitary condition of this institution now and during the year, as shown by the Physician's report, also the interesting statements of the Chaplain, and his views on "punishment;" thankfully acknowledging the goodness and guidance of God in all that relates to our administration, your own kind confidence always extended to me, and the cheerful co-operation and valuable assistance of the "assistants" generally; we enter upon the new year amidst the difficulties arising from the recent calamity hoping that the effort to *overcome* may be successful, and the prosperity and usefulness of our institution with its adjuncts, be established and enlarged.   Your obedient servant,

Z. R. BROCKWAY,
Superintendent.

December 31, 1870.

INCOME.

CHAIR ACCOUNT.

Stock, tools and machinery on hand Jan. 1, 1870,	$62,556 92	
Charged this account for services of principal foreman and for work furnished by the several departments,............	134,528 07	
Charged the several departments of this account for stock, tools, services of foreman and overseers, and for labor of citizens,....	84,214 58	
		$281,299 57
Amount credited this account for chairs sold,....	$146,153 42	
Amount credited the different departments of this account for work furnished by them..........	121,760 22	
Stock, tools and machinery on hand December 31, 1870, previous to the fire.... ....*	69,686 75	
		337,600 39
Balance to the credit of chair account............		$56,300 82

BOARD ACCOUNT.

Received and charged for board of prisoners from Wayne County, ... $3,835 96		
Less for 75 per cent. of the amount charged to board account and credited to stock account, that being the approximate ratio of the county taxes for 1870 assessed upon the wards of the city,.... .... 2,876 97		
	$958 99	
Received and charged for board of prisoners other than those from Wayne County....	12,128 48	
		$13,087 47

SHOE SHOP ACCOUNT.

Received and charged for labor of prisoners..............		2,112 59
Total income		$71,500 88

EXPENDITURE.

GENERAL EXPENSE ACCOUNT.

Property on hand January 1, 1870	$3,233 22	
Total expended during the year for salaries, fuel, lights, and other general expenses	28,248 50	
		$31,481 72
Amount credited this account for ashes and a horse sold	$881 79	
Property on hand December 31, 1870..	4,239 61	
		5,121 40
Leaving for amount expended.......................		$26,360 32

CLOTHING AND BEDDING ACCOUNT.

Property on hand January 1, 1870,....	$4,983 65	
Amount purchased since.............	5,806 66	
		$10,790 31
Amount credited this account	$153 21	
Property on hand December 31, 1870..	5,506 62	
		5,659 83
Leaving for amount expended.................		$5,130 48

PROVISION ACCOUNT.

Provisions on hand January 1, 1870...	$1,761 19	
Amount purchased since.............	19,544 63	
		$21,305 82
Amount credited this account	$451 55	
Property on hand December 31, 1870,.	1,004 18	
		1,455 73
Leaving for amount expended		$19,850 09

FURNITURE AND FIXTURES ACCOUNT.

Property on hand January 1, 1870....	$7,863 91	
Amount purchased since.............	3,232 39	
		$11,096 30
Amount credited this account	$208 51	
Property on hand December 31, 1870..	9,300 78	
		9,509 29
Leaving for amount expended.....................		$1,587 01

REPAIRS ACCOUNT.

Repairs to the cornice along the whole line of building,	$ 695 69	
Rebuilding and enlarging brick oven,	105 90	
Repairing roofs (slating, cementing, tinning, and carpenter work),	418 24	
Painting the whole establishment inside,	792 10	
Relaying floors,	609 65	
Iron gratings, doors, wire work and bell hanging.	343 76	
Blinds for shops and hospital, window strips, etc,,	209 89	
Nursery stock for the large vegetable garden,	214 00	
Trees, shrubs, and work on grounds,	329 91	
Repairing high fence around rear grounds, stairway to old cane shop, and repairs to female workshop,	368 69	
Steam and gas fitting repairs,	614 18	
Locks, nails, latches, screws, water-lime, and sundry matters of repair,	676 32	
		$5,378 33

HOUSE OF SHELTER ACCOUNT.

Property on hand January 1, 1870,	$2,006 89		
Since expended for maintenance and repairs,	1,574 92		
		$3,581 81	
Amount credited for work done,	$316 93		
Property on hand Dec. 31, 1870,	1,761 87		
		2,078 80	
			1,503 01

DISCHARGED PRISONERS ACCOUNT.

Paid to railroads for fare of discharged prisoners to the place from whence they came,	$351 40	
Gratuities to prisoners on their release, to aid them in procuring temporary sustenance, disbursed in sums from 25c. to $10	886 24	
Paid prisoners on their release, in consideration of special and responsible service,	128 00	
		$1,365 64
Amount paid for insurance,		1,194 50
Amount paid for interest,		2.520 69
Doubtful accounts (from Suspense account),		1,286 17
Total expenditure,		$66,176 24

RECAPITULATION.

INCOME.

Chair Account,................	$56,300 82	
Board Account,.....	13,087 47	
Shoe Shop Account,.....	2,112 59	
		$71,500 88

EXPENDITURE.

General Expense account,.....	$26,360 32	
Clothing and Bedding Account, ...	5,130 48	
Provision Account,.....	19,850 09	
Furniture and Fixtures Account,.....	1,587 01	
Repairs Account, ...	5,378 33	
House of Shelter,.....	1,503 01	
Discharged Prisoners Account,.....	1,365 64	
Insurance Account, ...	1,194 50	
Interest Account,.....	2,520 69	
Suspense Account,.....	1,286 17	
		66,176 24

*Amount gained to the institution during the year.... $5,324 64

* The amount of loss by fire (exclusive of the building) over and above insurance is $7,013.26, which is carried to stock account subsequent to the above closing of the accounts, and changes of course the result stated above to a *deficit* of $1,688.92.

STATEMENT OF PROPERTY.

JANUARY 1, 1870.

Furniture and Fixtures,............................	$7,863 91	
Clothing and Bedding, ...	4,983 65	
General Expenses,.................................	3,233 22	
Provision Account, ...	1,761 19	
Chair Account, ...	62,556 92	
House of Shelter,.................................	2,006 89	
		$82,405 78

DECEMBER 31, 1870.

Furniture and Fixtures,............................	$9,300 78	
Clothing and Bedding, ...	5,506 62	
General Expenses,.................................	4,239 61	
Provision Account, ...	1,004 18	
*Chair Account,...................................	69,686 75	
House of Shelter,.................................	1,761 87	
		$91,499 81
Increase,..		$9,094 03

* The amount of property in the department Chair Account is reduced by the fire 31s, December, 1870, to $50,673.49, and the aggregate of property at this date to $72,486.55, showing a *decrease* (instead of an increase) of $9,909.23.

COMPARATIVE STATEMENT OF CASH, DEBTS AND PROPERTY.

Cash on hand 1st January, 1870, ... $2,900 77
Cash overdrawn 31st December, 1870,   2,676 78

  Decrement, ... $5,577 55
Balance of debts against the institution
 1st January, 1870, as reported,..... $19,899 85
Balance of debts against the institution
 December 31, 1870, ...   22,209 98

  Decrement, ...   2,310 13
Credited Stock Account and charged Board Account
 75 per cent of the amount received and charged
 for Board of Prisoners from Wayne county during the year,..........................   2,876 97
Amount gained to the institution and carried to
 Stock Account *exclusive* of the loss by fire,....   *5,324 64

  Total decrement, ... $16,089 29
Amount of property on hand January 1,
 1870, ...$82,405 78
Amount of property on hand 31st De-
 cember, 1870, *previous to the fire,*...   91,499 81

  Increase,............................. $9,094 03
Amount expended for permanent building and
 other permanent improvements, viz :
To complete the north wing,......... $5,007 58
For additional heating apparatus,.....   467 84
For the shipping house, including the
 roof and platform,................   288 52
For roads and walks,................   764 89
To increase height of yard wall,......   466 43
         ———————   6,995 26

  Total, ... $16,089 29

 * The entries subsequently made covering the loss on Stock, Tools and Machinery
by the fire which occurred in the last hours of the 31st December, 1870, changes this item
of gain to a loss over insurance and over this gain, of $1,688.62.

SUMMARY.

Balance to the credit of Stock Account,..........	$66,613 05	
Ledger balances and bills payable.	54,144 83	
Cash overdrawn, ...	2,676 78	
		$123,434 66
Inventory of personal property,.................	$91,499 81	
Bills and accounts receivable,....	31,934 85	
		$123,434 66

The entries subsequent to the fire, necessitated by it, change this statement as follows, viz :

Balance to the credit of Stock Account,..........	$59,599 79	
Ledger balances and bills payable, ...	54,144 83	
Cash overdrawn, ...	2,676 78	
		$116,421 40
Inventory of personal property,.................	$72,486 55	
Bills and accounts receivable,....	43,934 85	
		$116,421 40

STATEMENT OF THE FINANCIAL RESULT FOR EACH YEAR OF THE INSTITUTION.

	Deficit.	Surplus.
For the sixteen months ending December 31, 1862,	$9,242 34	....
For the year ending December 31, 1863,..........	2,237 80	....
" " " 1864,........	....	$2,011 80
" " " 1865,........	....	10,097 27
" " " 1866,....	....	20,108 32
" " " 1867,........	....	20,027 50
" " " 1868,........	....	15,203 37
" " " 1869,........	.. ..	13,869 71
" " " 1870,....	....	5,324 64
	$11,480 14	$86,642 61
		11,480 14
Excess of surplus over deficit for the nine years, ...		$75,162 47

The loss by fire this year on machinery, tools and manufacturing stock is, over and above insurance,....	$7,013 26

Leaving still a surplus of earnings for the whole period of the Institution, ...	$68,149 21

STATEMENT OF PRISONERS.

Number in confinement January 1, 1870,.................. 425
Number received from Jan. 1, 1870, to Dec. 31, 1870, inclusive,. 1,165

Whole number in confinement during the year, ... 1,590
Discharged by expiration of sentence,..................... 910
Procured bail,....................................‥‥..... 55
Payment of Penalty, ... 198
Habeas Corpus,... 4
Pardoned, ... 7
Escaped,.. 4
Died,:.. 6
On Appeal,.. 4
Order of Court,... 35
Order of Board of Inspectors,............................. 14

Total, ... 1,237

REMAINING IN CONFINEMENT DECEMBER 31, 1870.

Male Prisoners, ... 254
Female Prisoners, ... 99

Total,.. 353

NUMBER RECEIVED EACH MONTH.

	Males.	Females.	Total.
January, ...	56	12	68
February, ...	59	13	72
March,...	70	19	89
April, ...	73	26	99
May,...............	83	24	107
June, ...	103	27	130
July,...............	72	27	99
August, ...	88	37	125
September,..........	75	22	97
October,............	56	22	78
November, ...	70	12	82
December,...........	97	22	119
	902	263	1,165

NUMBER REMAINING AT THE END OF EACH MONTH.

	Males.	Females.	Total.
January,	318	109	427
February,	316	96	412
March,	308	98	406
April,	267	104	371
May,	237	111	348
June,	254	113	367
July,	246	112	358
August,	253	114	367
September,	241	111	352
October,	206	111	317
November,	212	88	300
December,	254	99	353
	3,112	1,266	4,378

MONTHLY AVERAGE IN CONFINEMENT DURING THE YEAR.

Males,	$259\frac{4}{12}$
Females,	$105\frac{6}{12}$
Total,	$364\frac{10}{12}$

BY WHOM OR FROM WHERE THOSE RECEIVED DURING THE YEAR WERE COMMITTED.

Julius Stoll, City of Detroit,	336
A. G. Boynton, City of Detroit,	331
Recorder's Court, City of Detroit,	25
Circuit Court,	4
United States Court, Michigan,	3
United States Court, Nebraska,	2
Wyoming Territory,	10
Justices of the Peace of Wayne county,	56
Alpena county,	3
Bay county,	28
Berrien county,	9
Branch county,	16
Calhoun county,	24
Cass county,	5
Eaton county,	5
Geneseo county,	19
Hillsdale county,	6
Houghton county,	1
Ingham county,	8
Jackson county,	69

Kent county,...   3
Kalamazoo county,...   24
Lenawee county,,,..   25
Livingston county,..   1
Macomb county,...   6
Monroe county,...   9
Montcalm county,...   2
Muskegon county,...   1
Midland county,...   1
Oakland county,...:....   9
Ottawa county,...........................   5
Saginaw county,.............................,................   54
St. Clair county, ...   7
St, Joseph county,...   3
Washtenaw county,..   55
                                                        —— 1,165
Received from the City of Detroit,..................   696
Elsewhere,...   469
                                                        —— 1,165

SENTENCES OF PRISONERS RECEIVED DURING 1870.

Twenty years,..	1	Eighty-five days,..............	2
Ten years, ...	1	Eighty days, ...	1
Seven years,.................	1	Seventy-five days,............	2
Six years, ...	1	Seventy days, ...	2
Five years,...................	3	Sixty five days, ...	31
Four years,...................	2	Six months' imprisonment or a	
Three years and six months,...	3	fine, ...	122
Three years,.................	10	Ninety days to six months' im-	
Two years and six months, ...	1	prisonment or a fine,.......	180
Two years, ...	10	Thirty to ninety days' imprison-	
One year and six months,......	1	ment or a fine,............	307
One year, ...	36	Ten to thirty days' imprisonment	
Nine months,.................	3	or a fine, ...	60
Six months,.................	25	In default of bail for good be-	
Four months,.................	6	havior,....................	133
Three months or ninety days,..	150	Until twenty-one years of age..	1
Two months or sixty days,.....	59		
One month or thirty days, ...	9		1,165
One hundred and eighty days,..	2		

PREVIOUS OCCUPATION.

Artist, ...	1	Masons,....	9
Brewer,....	1	Machinists,...................	16
Bakers, ...	3	Moulders, ...	12
Barbers, ...	15	Merchants,...................	2
Bartenders,..................	3	Millers, ...	2

Bootblacks,	4	Miners,	2
Boiler makers,	7	Musician,	1
Bookkeepers,	7	No occupation,	25
Bricklayers,	9	Nail cutter,	1
Butchers,	9	Painters,	32
Blacksmiths,	16	Peddlers,	11
Broom maker,	1	Printers,	7
Beggar,	1	Porter,	1
Book binder,	1	Plaster cast maker,	1
Basket makers,	2	Physicians,	5
Cane seaters,	2	Reporter,	1
Cabinet makers,	4	Roofer,	1
Chair makers,	2	Railroad men,	8
Cigar makers,	7	Rag picker,	1
Clerks,	14	Servants and Housekeepers,	226
Coopers,	7	Sailors,	102
Carpenters,	38	Soldiers,	5
Cooks,	13	Seamstresses,	18
Chimneysweep,	1	Shoemakers,	25
Confectioners,	2	Stone cutters,	3
Carver,	1	Saloon keepers,	15
Dentists,	2	Showmen,	2
Draymen,	5	Sawyer,	1
Engineers,	6	Steel finisher,	1
Farmers,	100	Tinsmiths,	4
Firemen,	10	Tailors,	4
Fisherman,	1	Teachers,	2
Filecutter,	1	Tanner,	1
Glassblowers,	2	Traveling agents,	10
Gardeners,	3	Turner,	1
Gas fitters,	3	Upholsterers,	2
Hostlers and Teamsters,	29	Umbrella maker,	1
Harness makers,	3	Whitewashers,	2
Hack drivers,	2	Waiters,	5
Hotel runner,	1	Washerwomen,	5
Hatters,	3	Wagon makers,	2
Laborers,	243		
Lumbermen,	5	Total,	1,165

Educated Professions,	17
Artizans,	155
Laborers, servants and miscellaneous,	993
	1,165

NATIVITY.

At Sea,	3	Novia Scotia,	1
Alabama,	1	New Hampshire,	1
Austria,	2	New York,	199
Arkansas,	3	Newfoundland,	1
Belgium,	2	North Carolina,	1
Canada,	141	New Brunswick,	3
Connecticut,	5	Ohio,	45
District of Columbia,	3	Pennsylvania,	24
England,	63	Prussia,	8
France,	6	Portugal,	1
Florida,	1	Rhode Island,	2
Germany,	77	Scotland,	37
Georgia,	2	South America,	1
Holland,	5	South Carolina,	2
Illinois,	6	Spain,	1
Indiana,	11	Sweden,	2
Ireland,	234	Switzerland,	3
Italy,	2	Texas,	1
Kentucky,	19	Tennessee,	4
Michigan,	179	Virginia,	19
Mississippi,	1	Vermont,	4
Maine,	4	West Indies,	1
Maryland,	4	Wisconsin,	2
Massachusetts,	12		
Missouri,	7	Total,	1,165
New Jersey,	9		

Foreign born, ... 453
Native, ... 712
— 1 165

CRIME OR OFFENSE.

Assault, ... 16
Assault and battery, ... 55
Assault with intent to kill, ... 2
Administering poison with intent to kill, ... 1
Abandoning a child, ... 1
Adultery, ... 5
Arson, ... 1
Burglary, ... 4
Burglary and larceny, ... 2
Bigamy, ... 1
Conspiracy, ... 1
Drunkenness, ... 434
Disorderly, ... 284
Embezzlement, ... 1
False pretenses, ... 1
Forgery, ... 4

Indecent exposure, ... 4
Keeping House of Ill-fame, ... 5
Larceny (simple), ... 212
Larceny (grand), ... 16
Malicious trespass, ... 4
Manslaughter, ... 6
Passing counterfeit U. S. currency,................., ... 2
Robbing U. S. mail, ... 2
Robbery, ... 1
Riot, ... 1
Receiving stolen goods, ... 1
Selling liquors without license, ... 1
Threats, ... 8
Violation of hack ordinances, ... 1
Vagrants, ... 88
                                                        ——
       Total, ...1,165
Offenses against the person, ... 82
Offenses against property, ... 481
Offences against the peace, ... 602
                                                        —— 1,165

SOCIAL RELATION.

Married and having children, ... 306
Married and having no children, ... 132
Unmarried and having both parents, ... 283
Unmarried and having only one parent, ... 158
Widows or widowers having children, ... 42
No relation, ... 244
                                                        ——
       Total, ...1,165
Living in family relation, ... 434
Living out of family relation, ... 731
                                                        —— 1,165

EDUCATION.

Could read and write, ... 738
Could read only, ... 203
Could neither read nor write, ... 224
                                                        —— 1,165

AGE WHEN ADMITTED.

Under 20 years of age, ... 212
From 20 to 25 years of age, ... 231
From 25 to 30 years of age, ... 202
From 30 to 40 years of age, ... 301
From 40 to 50 years of age, ... 131
Fifty years of age and over, ... 88
                                                        —— 1,165

RELIGIOUS TRAINING.

Roman Catholics,	494
Protestants,	631
Without religious training,	40
	—— 1,165

HABITS OF LIFE.

Claim to be temperate,	301
Admit themselves to be intemperate,	864
	—— 1,165

COLOR.

White,	1,043
Black,	122
	—— 1,165

PREVIOUS CONVICTION.

Recommitted once,	179
Recommitted twice,	74
Recommitted three times,	48
Recommitted four times,	22
Recommitted five times,	16
Recommitted six times,	12
Recommitted eight times,	3
Recommitted nine times,	4
Recommitted ten times,	4
Received for the first time,	803
	—— 1,165

TABLE SHOWING THE LENGTH OF TIME THE INMATES WHO HAVE BEEN DISCHARGED DURING THE YEAR 1870 ACTUALLY REMAINED IN THE INSTITUTION.

Forty-four months,	1	Nine months,	9
Thirty-six months,	1	Eight months,	5
Thirty-five months,	2	Seven months,	7
Thirty-three months,	1	Six months,	216
Thirty-two months,	4	Five months,	26
Thirty one months,	1	Four months,	53
Twenty-eight months,	1	Three months,	241
Twenty-five months,	1	Two months,	175
Twenty-four months,	1	One month,	144
Twenty-two months,	2	Twenty to fifteen days,	24
Twenty-one months,	1	Fifteen to ten days,	30
Eighteen months,	4	Ten to five days,	27
Sixteen months,	1	Five days and less,	162
Twelve months,	56		——
Eleven months,	34	Total,	1,237
Ten months,	7		

Average time those discharged during the year actually remained in confinement ....114 days.

TABLE

SHOWING THE LOSS AND GAIN IN THE WEIGHT OF PRISONERS DURING
THEIR TERM OF IMPRISONMENT, UNDER FOUR CLASSIFICATIONS OF
SENTENCE.

TIME IMPRISONED.	Number weighed.	Increase.	Decrease.	Balance of increase over decrease.	Average Increase over decrease.	Largest single increase.	Largest single decrease.
MALES—					lbs. oz.		
Less than thirty days	14	49	6	43	3 1	12	3
From thirty to ninety days	191	769	171	598	3 2	29	15
From ninety days to six months ..	155	615	200	415	2 11	21	15
From six months to one year	153	739	309	430	2 13	31	18
Total Males	513	2,172	686	1,486	...	....	....
FEMALES—							
Less than thirty days..............	3	12	....	12	4	7	....
From thirty to ninety days	19	114	13	101	5 5	12	6
From ninety days to six months ..	35	199	55	144	4 2	19	11
From six months to one year	62	466	120	346	5 9	37	12
Total Females	119	791	188	603	....	....	....
Grand Total....................	632	2,963	874	2,089	3 5	....	....

TEACHER'S REPORT.

During the past year the evening school for the instruction of inmates of the House of Correction, has become established on a broader basis than before, and what was at first a doubtful experiment has become an assured success.

Though basis of organization and methods of management are doubtless susceptible of much improvement, still we now feel confident that our methods are at least uesful; while in the beginning of the enterprise we groped our way, testing every step.

The effort of the school has been to give each man so far as possible a knowledge of reading, of writing, and of numbers. We cannot boast of having produced any remarkable scholars; but we have abundant evidence that a large majority of the men have felt themselves greatly profited by the educational advantages here afforded. Our programme of exercises has included singing, led by Miss Hall, followed by a fifteen minutes address on some educational topic by myself, after which the class recitations for the evening have been conducted almost exclusively by prisoners selected for this work; though it is proper to say that Mr. M. W. Mahony, an officer of the House, has afforded very satisfactory assistance in this work during the entire year.

The lessons have been prepared in the cells.

ENROLLMENT.

There were enrolled January 1st, 1870	106
There have been since enrolled	272
Making total enrollment	378
Of these there have left	258
Leaving on the rolls at date	120

There have been 84 sessions of 2½ hours each, with an average attendance of 97. The average number of sessions each man has attended is 22; showing that we have virtually 4 sets of pupils per year. The changes of teachers have not been in the same ratio, but still have been too numerous for profit, 22 different men having had charge of an average of 8 classes. This difficulty will be in a measure obviated as the *long term* men become qualified to act as teachers. The 5 classes with which we commenced the year have increased by subdivisions and closer grading to 12; and had we suitable places in which to seat them, it would be advisable to increase the number of classes until no more that 6 or 7 pupils were in the charge of a single teacher.

CLASSIFICATION.

Those now belonging are classified in reading as follows:

In Word Method	6
" Second Reader	14
" Fourth Reader	84
" Fifth Reader	16
	120

There are using Stoddard's Practical Arithmetic	78
" " " " Intellectual "	81
" " receiving oral instruction only	20

The education of the men received at this House may be judged from the following statement showing the text-book knowledge on admission, compared with pupils in our public schools. Those not familiar with the grading of the schools in this city will get the most definite idea of the scholarship indicated, by considering that the Primary Grade comprises the first two years of school work, usually done by pupils of 6 to 8 years of age; the Secondary Grade comprises the second two years, age of pupils 8 to 10; the Junior Grade comprises the third two years, age of pupils 10 to 12; the Senior Grade comprises the seventh, eighth and ninth years of school work, age of pupils 12 to 15.

Thus computed, the scholarship of those admitted is as follows :

33 per cent. correspond to pupils of the Primary Grade.
21   "   "   "   "   Secondary   "
35   "   "   "   "   Junior   "
11   "   "   "   "   Senior   "
     and more advanced.

The present educational status of the men may be judged from the following table, showing the correspondence in text-book acquirements between pupils now in attendance in the House of Correction School, and those of the Public Schools.

16 per cent. correspond to those of the Primary Grade
20   "   "   "   "   Secondary   "
50   "   "   "   "   Junior   "
14   "   "   "   "   Senior   "
     and more advanced.

PROGRESS.

Of those whose names are on our rolls for January 1st, 1870, there are at this date enrolled 14, one (the first of those whose progress is specified below) by virtue of recommitment, the others by duration of sentence. I know not how I can more briefly or fairly give a view of the progress of the members of the school than by detailing the advancement of each of these men, whom I consider correct representatives of the whole number, and who are selected only because their period of attendance (one year) renders them the most convenient for the purpose.

For a standard of measurement I shall refer their progress to the advancment made in one year in the Public Schools by pupils in the same studies.

Thus judged, of this number, during the 84 sessions or less attended,

1 has learned nothing.
1 has done 1 year's school work.
8 have done 2 years' school work each.
3 have done 3½ years' school work each.
1 has done 4 years' school work.
――   ――
14 averaging 2½ years' school work each.

I think it is within bounds to say that the men have, on the average, learned twice as much per week with instruction on 2 evenings only, as children in the Public Schools with 5 days' instruction per week.

Since Nov. 9th, a writing school of an hour's duration, two evenings per week, has been conducted by officer Mahony with much success. From an examination made by Prof. Nichols, of the Cass School, and myself, it was decided that the men were making more than twice the advancement of Public School children under the best teachers. I know not where a pleasanter sight to the eye of the professional teacher or philanthropist can be found than the writing school in the Detroit House of Correction.

But while a very definite statistical statement of progress, both absolute and comparative, in that portion of education to be obtained from text-books and school drill may be made, and thus a faithful representation of that aspect of our school work be afforded, it is hard to place upon paper any adequate view of the plainly discernible change, which no figures can show, in the bearing of the men, their awakened desires for knowledge and self-culture, and their increased susceptibility to intellectual and moral truth.

I can only here express the conviction that at least nine-tenths become imbued, for the time being at least, with an earnest desire for knowledge and self-improvement, and that they are as successful in the accomplishment of this desire as can be reasonably expected of men so situated.

Respectfully submitted.

H. S. TARBELL,
Teacher.

DETROIT, December 31, 1870.

TEACHER'S REPORT.

(FEMALE DEPARTMENT).

It affords me pleasure at the close of another year to present you a brief statement of the progress made in our school, at present occupying four evenings of each week, two of them being given to exercises in reading, orthography and arithmetic, the two remaining to exercises in writing and singing.

I would acknowledge the kindly support and assistance of the other ladies and persons in charge in the institution, and the frequent, generous volunteer aid from the Superintendent's family; also the very efficient services as teachers rendered by four of the regular members of the school.

Two of these entered elementary classes at the opening of the school, two years ago, and have fitted themselves for assistants by their diligent application to the study of text books and methods of teaching, and an exemplary prison life.

The efforts for others on the part of these four teachers has proved an eminent but unconscious means of self help, they having experienced a marked mental and moral growth. Their success also acts upon others as a stimulus to similar exertion.

There have been 234 persons in school during the year, 74 of them having received instruction in the previous year; their progress making a perceptible difference in the percentage of the accompanying tables for the present year.

The previous acquirements of these 234 pupils are so varied, and there are so many degrees of ability and desire to learn, that it is an exceedingly difficult task to give a full and true idea of the real work accomplished. There are many instances of remarkable progress, and the *general* progress has been much greater than last year. There are three reasons for this increased progress: 1st. The school is an established fact. 2d. It it better classified and there are more assistants. 3d. There are a greater number of stimulating forces, viz. : lectures, readings, increased and improved library, music, etc.

The average condition of ignorance of those actually re-received is the same as that of last year.

The whole number in school, in 1869, was 224, or 61.54 per cent. of the prisoners.

The whole number in school, in 1870, was 234, or 64.64 per cent. of the prisoners.

All who were not in school were invalids, or occupied with necessary domestic duties, or were released before entering school by payment of penalties, &c., immediately after their admission. We had 74 pupils belonging at the close of 1869 and precisely the same number at the close of 1870. The average attendance at each session was 58 in 1869 and 68 in 1870, an increase of 10. The age of the pupils varies each year from 10 to 50, the average age being 24 years. The smallest number of sessions attended by any pupil is 3 each year; the largest number, 151 in 1869 and 98 in 1870; the average number of sessions of all the pupils is 36 in 1869 and 31 in 1870. This variation occurs from the fact that in 1869 we held 3 sessions per week, while in 1870 we held but 2 per week of the regular school, writing exercises, when given, being on the other evenings.

The following is, as far as it can well be made, a comparative statement of progress for the years 1869 and 1870 :

CONDITION IN READING.

	1869. Per cent.	1870. Per cent.
Could not read on admission to the school,	46.00	28.02
Could read, but with difficulty,	54.00	
Began in Second Reader,		21.08
Began in Third Reader,		24 03
Began in Fourth Reader		25.07

Progress in reading, at date of leaving school, or at date of this report :

			1869.	1870.
Reading readily in Fifth Reader,				20.65
"	"	Fourth Reader,	29.00	37.56
"	"	Third Reader,	31.25	17.00
"	"	Second Reader,	36.61	16.24
"	"	Webb's Word Method	3.14	8.55

4

CONDITION IN ARITHMETIC.

Could not add small numbers, and many could not count,...	88.35	65.53
Could add and subtract a little, but not able to multiply,....	10.19	11.11
Began with Practical Arithmetic,..........................		21.79
Had made some progress in Fractions,...................	1.46	1.67

Progress in arithmetic, at date of leaving school or at date of this report:

In percentage, Practical Arithmetic (and teacher's),........		3.42
In Fractions, " " " "	9.71	14.53
In Long Division, " " " "	34.00	20.53
In Multiplication, Intellectual Arithmetic,................	13.59	34.19
In Addition and Subtraction,...........................	42.70	28.33

The plan of instruction pursued in arithmetic has been:

1st.   Oral and Blackboard, or Slate exercises, for those unable to read.
2d.   Stoddard's Intellectual, as far as Division.
3d.   Practical Arithmetic begun and Intellectual continued.

CONDITION IN WRITING.

Could not write at all on admission to the school,..........	82.11	61.11
Could write, but very poorly,............................	17.89	23.50
Could conduct ordinary correspondence,...................		15.39

Progress in writing, at date of leaving school, or at date of this report:

Able to conduct ordinary correspondence,.................	43.71	27.77
Able to write a fair copy................................	56.29	55.12
Pupils have received no writing lessons..................		17.11

These figures indicate less progress in writing this year than in the previous one. The reason is this, viz.: the percentage is based upon the whole number of pupils in school, and a large number received no instruction in writing, since, at the beginning of the year, the writing class was discontinued for a season, when the school was removed to the new chapel, where the usual apparatus could not be furnished conveniently. Only slate exercises could be given to those most anxious to learn to write, until the class was reorganized 10th of November, 1870, the school-room having been refitted and refurnished with abundant light, and all the apparatus for a large, cheerful and convenient writing room. We use the Spencerian system of copy books; hence are able to classify the school readily, and secure a greater degree of progress, and economy of time and effort, and a better discipline than if we had not as correct a system.

The first half hour is given to singing exercises, consisting of both sacred and secular songs, accompanied by the organ. Then, for an hour, all apply themselves diligently to their writing. The quiet earnestness in the work, and the actual progress made in those fifteen lessons, indicate their real strength of purpose to acquire the difficult art of writing, and the mental acumen gained by this and the other educational means.

A ratio of merely text-book progress, obtained by assuming as a standard of comparison the advancement of a public school pupil in one year in the same branches, may assist in securing a fair judgment. Ninety-eight sessions, 2½ hours each, has been our school year. Of ten persons who have been here during the entire school year, or nearly so,

1 has done 1½ years' school work.
2 have done 2 years' school work.
5 have done 2½ years' school work.
2 have done 3½ years' school work.
—
10, averaging 2¾ years' school work.

There has been a steady, decided progress during the year, a gradually increased activity of mind, and ability to think and apply the faculties closely and continuously to a definite object.

A higher type of library books is chosen, and they are read more intelligently. There is a better and more critical reception of the lectures, addresses, and readings given them, and a perceptible seeking for practical helps to a better future life.

They are, according to the testimony of those in charge of them, better prisoners, and more skillful and industrious workers.

These facts, and a comparison of the experiences of persons whose history I have known subsequent to their discipline here, lead to the conviction that none should be deemed fitted to return to society until they are able to read and write well and keep their own accounts. They also demonstrate the possibility of the intellectual improvement of adult prisoners. They establish the fact that their *education*, in its broadest sense, will pay, and may be made to yield an hundred fold.

EMMA A. HALL.

DECEMBER 31, 1870.

CHAPLAIN'S REPORT.

To the Inspectors of the Detroit House of Correction:

GENTLEMEN—With the happy greetings of the New Year are mingled joyous remembrances, and grateful acknowledgments of the loving kindness of God vouchsafed to the House of Correction during the year now closed. Time would fail to enumerate the many pleasant, hopeful and good things that have been accomplished for, and secured to the inmates of our Reformatory. All the year long we have been borne to Heaven on the prayers of many loving hearts, who "remember those in adversity as being themselves in the flesh." We have been made joyous in song. We have been enriched by lectures and "readings." We have been rendered studious and content by the night schools. We have been cultured and instructed by good reading.* We have been edified and refreshed by our prayer and conversation meetings. We have been rendered doubly glad by the triumphs of the gospel over the lives of many who give evidence of being translated from the kingdom of darkness into the kingdom of God's dear Son. No Sabbath has passed during the year that has not been rendered memorable by numbers of these victories of grace.

By the constant application of these aids to reformation, the frowning severities of prison life have gradually faded away into the milder and more genial scenes of a home for the reformation of unfortunate criminals.

"I expected when I came here to be controlled by the "*iron rule*," said one of our inmates; "in place of which I have been bound by *moral* influences so strong that I think I shall never break away from them." Among the delights of the Chaplain's

---

* A special acknowledgment is due to Rev. A. T. Pierson for a large amount of literature of special utility, and highly prized by the prisoners.

vocation is the occasional meeting in the walks of life with the joyous faces of those to whom this retreat has been rendered "the power of God unto salvation."

Profoundly impressed with the belief that the *reformation* of depraved persons is infinitely more desirable than their punishment, the patient consideration of the Inspectors is earnestly solicited to the consideration of the question,

WHAT IS THE FIRST DUTY OF THE STATE TOWARDS THE VIOLATORS OF LAW?

A question in the solution of which the interests of such multitudes are involved, should be approached with the greatest care and the profoundest solicitude.

Probably in no age since the foundation of the world has so much thought been devoted to this subject as in our own. The wisest and most experienced men in christendom have spared no pains in their researches after light for the direction of their judgment in so grave a matter. And it is but just to the humane thinkers who have made this question a specialty, to say that they are well nigh unanimous in the opinion that a radical change in the action of the State towards its delinquents is demanded. Demanded not for the interest of the criminal only, but for the State as well.

If we speak boldly and confidently, we do not therefore speak presumptuously. We shall but utter the convictions that have been rendered profound by protracted thought and patient study. If we are "enthusiastic," it is the legitimate fruit of a confirmed faith.

We desire first of all not to be held to a false issue. The question to be considered is not punishment as against no punishment, but punishment as against, or in the place of, reformation.

What is the first duty of the State, to punish or to seek the reformation of the violator of law? Shall Justice or Mercy have the first chance with him? Shall he be given over to the enginery of pain and torture first, or shall the first appliances aim at his recovery to the paths of virtue and salvation? Does a sin that is not a "mortal sin" absolve the State from the duty to save men, that justice may have its "pound of flesh?" Shall mercy be denied her prerogative to staunch blood, lest the maw of justice be foiled of its precious morsel? The proposition involved in these questions is the one to be considered.

On the punitive side are arranged the following considerations:

"The criminal deserves or merits punishment as the rightful wages of his iniquity. Justice is defrauded if rightful retribution is withheld. Conscience, and the sense of justice innate with the offender, both demand and accept the punishment as appropriate and deserved, and nothing else will cover the sense of guilt. Punishment is demanded as a support to law. Law without penalty can neither prevent crime nor protect society."

"The *right* to punish is to be maintained against the sentimentalism which would substitute reformation for punishment."*

These considerations are certainly not without force, and it were a wrong to those controlled by them not to give them proper consideration. The first thought suggested by the above affirmations is that they demand of the State to become an eternal stranger, nay, an eternal enemy, to mercy.

If you sin you shall be punished, and that is the end of it. No matter who you are or what you are, there is no escape, be it the first offense or the last. Be the temptation what it may, or the aggravation, it is all the same. You shall receive just the number of stripes you *deserve*, no more, no less. Of pardons, there are none; of reprieves, you shall never hear, nor of commutation. To mercy we are strangers and enemies, in your disposition. We are after blood, and we will have blood and nothing but blood. The sword of Justice is sharp, and hungry for the repast. It shall not be cheated. Prepare the victim!

Are the advocates for punishment ready? Are they prepared to engraft such an article into their creed?

Shall the State neither show nor know mercy for the offender? Is there a domain on earth so large where Mercy never comes? Such was the universal sentiment prior to the advent of the immortal Howard. But, cruel as was this sentiment, it was based on reasons quite as philosophical as are modern reasons

---

* Moral Philosophy, by President Fairchild.

for denying to Mercy her heaven-born right to rejoice over Justice. Then it was said, "Reformation for the criminal is impossible; therefore let him be punished." Now it is said, crime demands its due;.therefore, let the exactor to his task.

But whole armies of reformed criminals have risen up to prove the falsity of the first assertion, and greater numbers shall yet come forth to demonstrate the sophistry of the second.

We now proceed to state a proposition, which we think will not be controverted. It is this: The State is bound to pursue that course towards criminals that will secure its own highest good. It is universally admitted that this is the principle on which God administers the government of this mundane system. And none need be informed that, in seeking this end, the first means in the Divine employ is the attempted *reformation* of offenders.

Now, if this is God's method for securing the greatest good, why should the State refuse to follow the Divine example? If infinite wisdom finds punishment, as the first experiment, not conducive to the end sought, why should the State render judgment, and pursue a practice in conflict with God? Is the State wiser than He? If God's first effort with the offender is for his recovery to obedience, is not here evidence presumptive of immense weight that it is also the wisest and best method for securing the best good of the State?

But it is insisted that "the criminal deserves punishment as the rightful wages of his iniquity." Granted. Yet, if the highest good of the State can be secured by cheating him out of his dues, then, for the sake of that good, he ought to be defrauded of what he deserves. If, in time of war, the State may sacrifice the lives of innocent citizens for its own preservation, how much more may the deserts of a criminal be withholden to secure the same end. God withholds from criminals their deserts that He may reform them; why not the State, also.

The advocates of vengeance are grieved, that by our philosophy of Reform, Justice should be robbed of her rights. To which we respond, that abstract justice is not to be regarded as an ultimate end in the treatment of criminals. If a higher good can be attained by supplanting justice with mercy, benevolence demands the change.

To administer justice to a sinner against the State is to impose stripes upon his quivering flesh, to take blood from his severed veins, or by some process to torture him with pain. It is this procedure that we insist should not be regarded as an ultimate end. Surely, neither the smell of blood nor the cry of pain should be more grateful to the State than the fragrance of virtue wrought by reformation. In the eyes of Heaven a "contrite heart is of great price," while judgment is a "strange work."

There is another standpoint from which this question of justice is to be viewed. It is this: The State has a property of intrinsic value in the offender, to be disposed of. Its first duty, after securing its own highest good, is to save to itself this amount of personal value. Any surrender of this duty to the claims of abstract justice is an injustice to itself.

The punitive philosophy places man in the second degree and justice in the first. We would reverse the order. With them, man was made for justice, not justice for man. What is this but a resurrection of the old Hebrew dogma, of the instrument first, and the subject afterwards; preserve the Sabbath, and let the man for whom it was made take care of himself. We have high authority for reversing this order.

But, we are reminded that the sense of justice which is innate with the criminal, and his conscience as well, do both demand and accept punishment, as appropriate and deserved.

To this proposition we both yield assent, and to the inference a total dissent. We know that crime and ill desert are inseparably correllated.

"Guiltiness would speak if tongues were out of use."
"The thief would deem each bush an officer."

And all this is as true of the offender against the Divine government, as of the offender against the State. But that either class demand punishment we deny. Did the Psalmist prefer such a demand for his offense when sending the imploring cry to heaven: "Cast me not away from Thy presence, take not Thy holy spirit from me." Was there a "demand" for punishment in the prayer of the Publican, " God be merciful to me a sinner ;" or, in the petition of the dying thief on the cross: " Remember me when Thou comest into Thy kingdom."

In the place of stripes, we ask that Government say to the offender: We pity the weakness that has beguiled and betrayed you into this offense; it will be for your good, and for ours, that you become a better man ; we will, therefore, help you to reform. In doing so we must restrain you for a season, that we may surround you with help to habits of virtue and industry. You have not yet learned that virtue brings her own reward, and vice its reward. It shall be ours to assist you. And when in the judgment of your teachers and guardians you have attained sufficient strength of will, and love of virtue, to withstand temptation, you shall be returned to the walks of society.

With the understanding that if the work of reformation is incomplete there will still be a vacancy for you in the school from which you were released.

We ask, at least, a trial for our method, as against the old one, under the influence of which, or in spite of which, crime in every form *is constantly increasing.**

Under the inspiration of the punitive philosophy ingenuity has been pressed to its utmost limit in inventing processes for repressing crime, and "inflicting justice on the criminal."

Men have been transported, attaindered, tortured to madness, gibbeted, shot, strangled, butchered, poisoned, starved, hung, drawn and quartered, roasted alive, and buried alive.†

And all this from the hands of those confessing themselves " miserable offenders !"

---

* *Interesting testimony—Letter of M. D. Hill, forty years Recorder of Birmingham, England, to the Cincinnati Prison Reform Congress :* " Having watched the operation of non-reformatory punishment for more than half a century, I can offer myself as a witness to the illusory nature of all expectation that they can be made effectual. My testimony, however, sinks into utter insignificance when compared with that of history, which, at every page, furnishes evidence leading to the same conclusion."

† Horace Walpole declares that he saw, from his carriage, a *cart load of girls going to execution !* And never, he adds, did I behold such weeping.

The question examined in the light of the Bible :

Whatever weight may attach to the above considerations, they are nevertheless powerless with those who think they find in the oracles of God a positive and irrevocable command, imposing on the State the obligation, not to reform but to punish criminals. For hearts thus loyal to the authority of God we have profound sympathy, and with them we surrender implicitly to the Divine will when known. With this concession we ask an unbiased attention to the following facts and suppositions :

1st. In given conditions of society God allows and sanctions usages, which in other and more advanced conditions He disallows.

Many practices received the Divine sanction, and were quite compatible with the state of early Jewish society, that were quite as incompatible with the status of Christian society.

It becomes legitimate now to inquire, may there not be such changes or higher grades of attainment in knowledge, philanthropy, and spirituality, such advances from the status of apostolic times, as to justify the abrogation of usages that then received the Divine sanction? Why not? Society did once and again make such progress as to justify God in abolishing laws and customs of his own ordaining. Who then shall say there are no higher attainments in the moral and political world; attainments that shall accrue to the benefit of the criminal classes.

We proceed now to prove that society has actually outgrown some of the usages that as clearly had the Divine sanction in the early Christian economy, as any sanction for the punitive treatment of criminals. The command for preaching with "uncovered heads" was as positive as for magistrates to execute wrath on evil doers. Who now addressing an outdoor audience, under a burning sun, or in a chilling wind, is deemed a violator of God's order if he neglect to "uncover." It is no more a question of obedience, but of convenience. The command had its origin in the then state of society, which state has given place to a higher. So also women, praying or speaking in public, were commanded to be vailed.

Now we know, that to vail the face in an assembly is to violate a physical law. Yet, to avoid a greater evil, it was then required. It was the sign of submission, says Albert Barnes. Who attaches such a "sign" to a vail now? It was also a sign of modesty says, the same expositor. But so universally is immodesty vailed in our day, that a distinguished minister of this city has adopted the rule never to return the salutation of a vailed stranger.

The progress of society has abolished the Divine law of vailing.

Take another case: In the apostolic instruction upon the marriage relation, Paul gives the following permission for sundering the conjugal bond: "If the unbelieving husband seek for a divorce it is not to be hindered, for in such cases the believing husband or wife are not bound to remain under the yoke." Such is the rendering of those eminent scholars, Conbeere and Howson.

But who now would risk his reputation on such advice or permission to an unbelieving husband, or a believing wife? The extreme religious antagonisms of those times have given place to a higher and better culture. And thus the necessity for such permission is gone.

We are now about to present an extreme case, demonstrating the proposition before us. But first let it be supposed that on the examination of that "cartload of girls," among them were found those who by reason of cruel treatment, extreme, and unjust suffering, or flagrant outrage from parental hands, had "cursed" their parents. Is there a sane man in all Christendom that would justify the taking of their lives for such an offense. And yet the Great Teacher himself quoted approvingly as against the Jews, the law of Moses, commanding the death of children for cursing their parents.

So few and feeble were the moral forces then in existence, that these extreme measures were the only means for averting universal anarchy. But with our relative advance in moral appliances, it is doubtful if a score of men in the entire commonwealth could be found to petition the Legislature to re-enact that ancient law. The progress of society has abolished the necessity.

Now if we are right in changing the Divine order in the above cases, we ask that the Bible may not be arrayed against us in the application of this principle to criminals.

The present status of society is radically different from theirs. Then the idea that a state criminal could be *reformed* had no place in their thoughts, nor were there appliances for such an achievement. They must therefore be put under the ban of hopeless exclusion or death. But how diverse the spirit of the present age. Now the criminal is regarded as our brother, an object of sympathy.* Bearing in himself the possibilities of endless felicity, concerning whom the question is coming more and more to be, not how much punishment shall be measured out to him, but by what possible means can his reformation and salvation be secured ?

Under the influence of this more excellent way, multitudes go forth from prison restraint to " sin no more " against the rights of society, but as conservators of public virtue. Once more we say, therefore, give our theory the chance of a trial. Every approximation to it has been crowned with triumphant success, both for the State and the criminal.†

Worthy of the profoundest reflection is the following solemn testimony of that eminent Christian philanthropist and scholar, Rev. Beriah Green, uttered nearly forty years ago : " Might I speak to the friends of improvement in prison discipline throughout this Republic, and throughout the world, with what deep

* An eminent divine, remarkable for the devoted piety and spotless purity of his character, was heard to say that he never read or heard of a crime in his life, no matter how heinous, without feeling an inward consciousness, that under certain conditions of education, he might have committed the same crime himself. The same feeling must have been experienced, more or less, by all reflecting and enlightened men ; and yet—and yet—how little charity there is in the world.

† See the experiment recently tried by the municipal authorities of Boston, namely, that of arresting criminal women, and suspending all sentence of the court against them until, by kindness and encouragement to reform, the strongest possible efforts had been made to reclaim them from vice. Of one hundred and thirteen thus arrested more than two-thirds returned to virtue's paths, either seeking their parents' home, respectable employment, or charitable asylums ; while since that, many others, of their own accord, have asked to be assisted in escaping from their dreadful bondage.

earnestness and strong emphasis would I say: Beware, as you would avoid utter and hopeless defeat in your designs, beware of excluding Jesus Christ from the sphere of your beneficent exertions. Without Him, you can do nothing to promote the permanent benefit of the objects of your kind regard. Slight the Savior, and you enter the penitentiary only to mock the prisoner and bring disgrace upon yourselves. Do ye not know —have ye not heard—have ye not *felt*, that 'Christ crucified is the power of God and wisdom of God to salvation,' to the loathsome criminal as well as the man of unblemished reputation ? In this warfare, away with 'carnal weapons,' wield the sword of the spirit; and, through Jesus Christ our Lord, you are more than conquerors !"

In conclusion the attention of the Inspectors is called to the suggestions in the Governor's Message, as to the inadequacy of salaries of prison officials, as not without application to this Institution.

Very respectfully,

C. C. FOOTE,
Chaplain.

PHYSICIAN'S REPORT.

To the Honorable Board of Inspectors of the Detroit House of Correction :

GENTLEMEN—In presenting you with a statement of the sanitary condition of the Detroit House of Correction during the past year, I am happy in being able to say that it compares favorably with any similar period since its establishment, the Hospital exhibiting on many occasions a "clean bill of health."

The necessary wants of the prisoners have been attended to with care, and their physical condition greatly improved during imprisonment by the strict enforcement of cleanliness, especially in being required to bathe always once a week, and during the warm season twice a week, for which abundant facilities are provided. They are generally cheerful and work willingly, thus rendering our curative means the more successful.

Six deaths have occurred during the year, of chronic disease, the most of them soon after being received here. The number of births, three.

We have nothing more to add to this brief report beyond a concluding record of reference to the Deputy Superintendent, Mr. Hugh B. Brockway, to whom acknowledgment is due. His perfect familiarity with the multiplied duties of his office from long experience, his ready and diligent co-operation at all times, has been to me an invaluable aid in the discharge of my duties.

Very respectfully yours,

JAMES A. BROWN,
Physician to House of Correction.

DETROIT, December 31, 1870.

www.ingramcontent.com/pod-product-compliance
Lightning Source LLC
Chambersburg PA
CBHW022031080426

42733CB00007B/801